Families Today

FOSTER FAMILIES

Families Today

Adoptive Families

Disability and Families

Foster Families

Homelessness and Families

Immigrant Families

Incarceration and Families

LGBT Families

Military Families

Multigenerational Families

Multiracial Families

Single-Parent Families

Teen Parents

Families Today

FOSTER FAMILIES

H.W. Poole

MASON CREST

Mason Crest
450 Parkway Drive, Suite D
Broomall, PA 19008
www.masoncrest.com

MTM Publishing, Inc.
435 West 23rd Street, #8C
New York, NY 10011
www.mtmpublishing.com

President: Valerie Tomaselli
Vice President, Book Development: Hilary Poole
Designer: Annemarie Redmond
Copyeditor: Peter Jaskowiak
Editorial Assistant: Andrea St. Aubin

Series ISBN: 978-1-4222-3612-3
Hardback ISBN: 978-1-4222-3615-4
E-Book ISBN: 978-1-4222-8259-5

Library of Congress Cataloging-in-Publication Data
Names: Poole, Hilary W., author.
Title: Foster families / by H.W. Poole.
Description: Broomall, PA : Mason Crest [2017] | Series: Families Today | Includes index.
Identifiers: LCCN 2016004541| ISBN 9781422236154 (hardback) | ISBN 9781422236123 (series) | ISBN 9781422282595 (e-book)
Subjects: LCSH: Foster home care—Juvenile literature. | Foster children—Juvenile literature. | Foster parents—Juvenile literature. | Families—Juvenile literature.
Classification: LCC HV873 .P66 2017 | DDC 362.73/3—dc23
LC record available at http://lccn.loc.gov/2016004541

Printed and bound in the United States of America.

First printing
9 8 7 6 5 4 3 2 1

TABLE OF CONTENTS

Key Icons to Look for:

Words to Understand: These words with their easy-to-understand definitions will increase the reader's understanding of the text, while building vocabulary skills.

Sidebars: This boxed material within the main text allows readers to build knowledge, gain insights, explore possibilities, and broaden their perspectives by weaving together additional information to provide realistic and holistic perspectives.

Research Projects: Readers are pointed toward areas of further inquiry connected to each chapter. Suggestions are provided for projects that encourage deeper research and analysis.

Text-Dependent Questions: These questions send the reader back to the text for more careful attention to the evidence presented there.

Series Glossary of Key Terms: This back-of-the-book glossary contains terminology used throughout the series. Words found here increase the reader's ability to read and comprehend higher-level books and articles in this field.

In the 21st century, families are more diverse than ever before.

SERIES INTRODUCTION

Our vision of "the traditional family" is not nearly as time-honored as one might think. The standard of a mom, a dad, and a couple of kids in a nice house with a white-picket fence is a relic of the 1950s—the heart of the baby boom era. The tumult of the Great Depression followed by a global war caused many Americans to long for safety and predictability—whether such stability was real or not. A newborn mass media was more than happy to serve up this image, in the form of TV shows like *Leave It To Beaver* and *The Adventures of Ozzie and Harriet*. Interestingly, even back in the "glory days" of the traditional family, things were never as simple as they seemed. For example, a number of the classic "traditional" family shows—such as *The Andy Griffith Show, My Three Sons,* and a bit later, *The Courtship of Eddie's Father*—were actually focused on single-parent families.

Sure enough, by the 1960s our image of the "perfect family" was already beginning to fray at the seams. The women's movement, the gay rights movement, and—perhaps more than any single factor—the advent of "no fault" divorce meant that the illusion of the Cleaver family would become harder and harder to maintain. By the early 21st century, only about 7 percent of all family households were traditional—defined as a married couple with children where *only* the father works outside the home.

As the number of these traditional families has declined, "nontraditional" arrangements have increased. There are more single parents, more gay and lesbian parents, and more grandparents raising grandchildren than ever before. Multiracial families—created either through interracial relationships or adoption—are also increasing. Meanwhile, the transition to an all-volunteer military force has meant that there are more kids growing up in military families than there were in the past. Each of these topics is treated in a separate volume in this set.

While some commentators bemoan the decline of the traditional family, others argue that, overall, the recognition of new family arrangements has brought more good than bad. After all, if very few people live like the Cleavers anyway, isn't it better to be honest about that fact? Surely, holding up the traditional family as an ideal to which all should aspire only serves to stigmatize kids whose lives differ from that standard. After all, no children can be held responsible for whatever family they find themselves in; all they can do is grow up as best they can. These books take the position that every family—no matter what it looks like—has the potential to be a successful family.

That being said, challenges and difficulties arise in every family, and nontraditional ones are no exception. For example, single parents tend to be less well off financially than married parents are, and this has long-term impacts on their children. Meanwhile, teenagers who become parents tend to let their educations suffer, which damages their income potential and career possibilities, as well as risking the future educational attainment of their babies. There are some 400,000 children in the foster care system at any given time. We know that the uncertainty of foster care creates real challenges when it comes to both education and emotional health.

Furthermore, some types of "nontraditional" families are ones we wish did not have to exist at all. For example, an estimated 1.6 million children experience homelessness at some point in their lives. At least 40 percent of homeless kids are lesbian, gay, bisexual, or transgender teens who were turned out of their homes because of their orientation. Meanwhile, the United States incarcerates more people than any other nation in the world—about 2.7 million kids (1 in 28) have an incarcerated parent. It would be absurd to pretend that such situations are not extremely stressful and, often, detrimental to kids who have to survive them.

The goal of this set, then, is twofold. First, we've tried to describe the history and shape of various nontraditional families in such a way that kids who aren't familiar with them will be able to not only understand, but empathize. We also present demographic information that may be useful for students who are dipping their toes into introductory sociology concepts.

Second, we have tried to speak specifically to the young people who are living in these nontraditional families. The series strives to address these kids as

Meeting challenges and overcoming them together can make families stronger.

sympathetically and supportively as possible. The volumes look at some of the typical problems that kids in these situations face, and where appropriate, they offer advice and tips for how these kids might get along better in whatever situation confronts them.

Obviously, no single book—whether on disability, the military, divorce, or some other topic—can hope to answer every question or address every problem. To that end, a "Further Reading" section at the back of each book attempts to offer some places to look next. We have also listed appropriate crisis hotlines, for anyone with a need more immediate than can be addressed by a library.

Whether your students have a project to complete or a problem to solve, we hope they will be able to find clear, empathic information about nontraditional families in these pages.

—H. W. Poole

The actors on the TV show *Modern Family* win awards for portraying a wacky-but-happy tribe. But real life is rarely that simple.

Chapter One

WHAT IS FOSTER CARE?

There are lots of shows about families on TV. Sometimes the dad is a goofball and the mom is a grouch. Sometimes the mom is fun but irresponsible, while the dad is calm but uptight. Either way, these shows have a lot in common with one another. Something goes wrong—maybe one of the kids gets in trouble, or maybe the parents disagree about something. But whatever the issue is, by the end of the show it all works out. In the world of these shows, there is no problem that can't be fixed in 30 minutes.

Of course, real life doesn't work like that. Sometimes parents just can't get along, no matter how hard they try. Sometimes there isn't enough money to

Words to Understand

disproportionate: when something is too large or too small in comparison to something else.

neglect: not taking care of something or someone.

reunification: putting something back together.

stereotype: a simplified idea about a type of person that is not connected to actual individuals.

pay rent or even buy dinner. Some parents have problems with drugs or alcohol. Some are either mentally or physically unwell. Others take out their problems on their kids by hurting them, either physically or with words.

Real life brings problems that can't be solved with a few jokes. And sometimes these problems mean that kids have to spend some time away from their families. Hopefully this only lasts a short while. But sometimes the separation is long, or even permanent. This is why the foster care system exists. Saying that someone is "in foster care" or "in the foster care system," means that the child is not living with his or her biological, or birth, parents. He or she is being looked after by someone else.

HOW DOES FOSTER CARE WORK?

Sometimes foster care is short-term. Let's say a single mom has two kids and needs to have an operation. If she doesn't have family who can help, the hospital

One example of temporary foster care would be if a single mom had to have a medical procedure; her child stays in foster care just while she is in the hospital, and they are reunited afterward.

might put her in touch with a social worker, who will help her find a place for the kids to stay. The mother will have her operation, recover in the hospital, and then the family will be reunited. In this example, foster care is a pretty easy and positive situation. The mom put her kids in care voluntarily, and she will get them back the minute she is ready.

This is called **reunification**. Child welfare laws in the United States are all based on the belief that most kids are better off with their birth parents. So the system is designed to keep as many families together as possible. Numbers vary from year to year, but about half of the kids in foster care end up going back to their parents.

Unfortunately, many foster situations are not as straightforward as this first example. If the state decides that a child is not safe at home, he or she is put in foster care, whether the parents like it or not. This can happen because of physical abuse, **neglect**, or for some other reason. For instance, if a single parent is arrested, the children might be put into foster care while the case is going on.

Foster care takes several different forms. Kids might be placed with relatives (called "kinship care"), in a group home, or with a foster family. (See chapter three for more on different types of foster care.) It is common for kids to experience a few different living situations while in foster care. For instance, the police might remove a child from an abusive home and put him or her into what's called "emergency" (short-term) care. That might last for a few days or a week, while social workers decide if it is safe for the child to return home. If it is not safe, the child will probably be moved to some other, hopefully more permanent, living situation.

FOSTER CARE BY THE NUMBERS

Because kids come and go, it is tricky to count how many foster kids there actually are. In any given period, say a month or a year, a certain number of kids will enter foster care, while a certain number of others will leave. They might return home, get adopted, or "age out" (a term referring to foster kids reaching adulthood, which is covered in chapter four).

It's Not Your Fault

It's easy for foster kids to blame themselves for the situation they're in. A kid might wonder why her parents didn't try harder to fix their problems, and might think, "Do they not love me enough?" Another kid might feel guilty that his parents "got in trouble" for not doing a good job. A foster kid might wonder, "If I behaved better, would my life be different?" Some kids feel guilty about being in foster care. Even if their parents abused them, they still feel like they should remain loyal, no matter what.

Sometimes parents have problems; it's not their kids' job to fix them.

All these feelings are understandable and natural. But it's *not* their fault. Children should not have to look after, protect, or rescue their parents. Kids are just kids! It's the parents' job to step up and do the right thing.

If your parents can't take care of you and you are moved into foster care, you have every right to feel sad or mad or even relieved. But however you feel, you are the kid, and you are not to blame.

One method is to pick a particular date and count how many kids there are in foster care on that single day. This is called a "point in time" survey. For example, on September 30, 2013, there were 402,378 children in U.S. foster care. That's a lot

More Foster Care Numbers

In the course of 2013:

- 255,000 kids entered the foster care system.
- 238,000 kids left the foster care system.
- 51,000 kids were adopted.
- 59,000 families terminated their parental rights (see chapter four for more on this concept).

of kids! The good news is that the number of kids in the foster system has been going down. On September 30, 2004, there were 517,000 kids in foster care. So, between 2004 and 2013 there was roughly a 20 percent drop.

Another way people count foster kids is the number of children "served" by the system. "Served" just means they were already in the system when the year began, *or* they entered during the year. For example, in 2013, there were 641,000 U.S. kids served. To give you an idea of how many people that is, it's roughly the same number as the estimated population of Boston.

WHO ARE FOSTER KIDS?

Some people believe that most foster kids are teenagers. But that **stereotype** is not correct. The average age of a foster child in 2013 was 8 years and 3 months old, and the average age of a child entering foster care for the first time was 6 years and 3 months old.

Other people believe that most foster kids are minorities, but that's not true, either. Foster kids come from all races and ethnic groups. The largest number of foster kids are white, followed by black, then Hispanic, Native American, and finally Asian.

That said, it's important to take a minute to understand these numbers. Yes, there are more white kids in foster care overall. But keep in mind that there are also more

The stereotype that foster kids are all in their teens is not true; the average age is between eight and nine years old.

white kids in the United States generally. The fact is, there are **disproportionate** numbers of both African-American and Native American kids in foster care.

A study by the National Council of Juvenile and Family Court Judges looked at this question in 2009. They found that while black kids made up 14 percent of the total population of American children, they were 30 percent of the total number of kids in foster care that year. The same study found that while Native American (including Alaska Native) kids are only 0.9 percent of the total population, they were 2 percent of the total number of kids in foster care. (The table on page 17 shows what those numbers looked like in 2013. Also see page 22 for more on Native Americans and foster care.)

One thing many foster kids have in common is poverty. For example, the *Milwaukee-Journal Sentinel* reported that in 1998, Wisconsin children whose parents earned $15,000 or less were *6 times* more likely to end up in foster care than kids whose parents had higher incomes.

FOSTER CARE BY RACE AND ETHNICITY, 2013

Race or ethnicity	Percentage of children in foster care	Percentage of children in United States
White (non-Hispanic)	42	54
Black (non-Hispanic)	24	14
Hispanic or Latino (any race)	22	23
American Indian (including Alaska Native)	2	1
Asian or Pacific Islander	1	5
Two or more races	6	4
Race unknown	3	--

Note: Percentages may not total 100 because of rounding.
Source: Children's Bureau (https://www.childwelfare.gov/pubPDFs/foster.pdf) and Child Trends Databank (http://www.childtrends.org/wp-content/uploads/2012/11/60_fig1a.jpg).

Text-Dependent Questions

1. What are some reasons why kids are in foster care?
2. How many kids left foster care in 2013?
3. Name one factor that might make it more likely for a child to need foster care.

Research Project

Look at the various statistics about children in foster care. The U.S. Department of Health and Human Services issued a report that is available online (go to http://www.acf.hhs.gov/sites/default/files/cb/afcarsreport21.pdf). Choose one of the tables and draw a bar chart or line graph that shows the statistics reported in it.

Street kids in New York City in 1910, photographed in the act of stealing from a fruit vendor.

Chapter Two

HISTORY OF FOSTER CARE

For a very long time, foster care was an informal thing. If you were a kid whose parents couldn't look after you, there was no authority to step in and help. You'd probably go live with a relative, or maybe with someone from your church. Some orphans ended up in institutions called almshouses. Others became **indentured servants**; they were sent over from England to work in the American colonies. Many just had to fend for themselves.

America's foster system started in New York City in the mid-19th century. The city's police commissioner was George W. Matsell, and in 1849 he published a report on homeless children. The Matsell Report estimated that there

Words to Understand

embryo: unborn, still developing.

federal: having to do with the central government, rather than the states.

incentive: something that encourages a person to do something.

indentured servant: a person who earns room and board by working for someone for a certain period of time.

permanence: the quality of being permanent, or not changing.

were 5,000 children on the city's streets. (Other estimates from the same era were far higher.)

Matsell said these kids were either "delinquent," meaning they didn't attend school, or "vagrant," which was a term for homeless. But many of the children probably did have homes. They might have been left unsupervised while their parents worked long hours. Or they might have been sent out by their parents to steal, beg, or sell matches and other small items. But Matsell argued that the "vagrant" and "delinquent" children of today were the criminals of tomorrow. In fact, he described them as "**embryo** felons."

Matsell wasn't alone in his worries. A number of different charities were established to try and help kids in poverty. For example, settlement houses were founded in many cities. They offered health care, educational opportunities, and other services to the poor. Some—such as Hull House in Chicago—also created a short-term, informal version of foster care.

THE ORPHAN TRAIN MOVEMENT

In 1853 a minister named Charles Loring Brace founded the Children's Aid Society (CAS) to help extremely poor and homeless children. As Brace declared in an editorial for *The New York Times*, "the outcast ragged boy shall find a home" (January 1, 1853). The CAS still exists; it is a respected charity that provides many services for New York City's underprivileged children.

One of Reverend Brace's biggest programs was the Orphan Train movement. Brace believed that poor city kids would be much better off with far-away Christian families, rather than left to survive on the streets. So, from 1854 to 1929, about 250,000 children were sent to live and work on farms across the United States. Many of them were not orphans at all; they were turned over by their parents for various reasons. And the children did not come only from New York. For example, the New England Home for Little Wanderers in Boston also sent children away on Orphan Trains.

Unlike foster placements today, almost no thought went into which children should go where. The train would head west, stopping at farming communities along the way. The children would be brought out for inspection. If a farmer saw one he liked, he would take the child home. No official records were kept about what happened to the children after they were taken off the train. Brace said that he wanted to send a representative to visit each family, but with so many families spread out over such a large country, few visits ever occurred. So we don't know if children were well cared for, if they were abused, or anything else about them. We do know that some of the kids, especially the older boys, simply ran away when they got the chance.

Some people were troubled by the Orphan Trains. The process of selecting a child reminded them of buying slaves. In fact, the Orphan Train movement gained popularity at the very same time that slavery was ending in the South.

Orphans in New York City, in the early 1900s. Many kids like these were sent out west as part of the Orphan Train movement.

Native American Children

We can all agree that children should be protected from abuse and neglect. But sometimes not everyone agrees on what "abuse and neglect" really means. For example, Native American families have suffered greatly from the racist view that their children would be better off raised in white families. Until the 1970s, as many as 35 percent of Native American children were removed from their parents and placed in group homes or with white foster parents.

The Indian Child Welfare Act (ICWA) was finally passed in 1978. It stated, "There is no resource that is more vital to the continued existence and integrity of Indian tribes than their children. . . . [And yet] an alarmingly high percentage of Indian families are broken up by the removal, often unwarranted, of their children from them by nontribal public and private agencies."' The ICWA declared that only tribal courts could determine whether it is truly necessary to remove a child from his or her home.

But according to the National Indian Child Welfare Association (NICWA), the removal of Native American kids continues at higher rates than white kids. (See page 15 for more on this concept.) In addition, families of other ethnic backgrounds are more likely to be offered parental training, counseling, and other help to try and keep the family together. The NICWA says that Native American kids are more likely to be removed from home as a "first resort," before other methods are tried.

A Southerner named J. H. Mills wrote, "men needing labor, their slaves being set free, take these [orphan] boys and treat them as slaves."

However, it was not a bad situation for every child. Many kids were adopted by their new families. Some of them did very well in life. For example, two future governors—Andrew Burke of North Dakota and John Green Brady of Alaska—rode the very same Orphan Train as boys. Other "Orphan Train riders" became ministers, journalists, lawyers, doctors, and so on. Alice Ayler, one of many children placed by Orphan Train, told an interviewer, "It hurt awfully bad, being separated from my family. But as I got older and realized, I would have never stood a chance if they had left me in that environment. I would never have gotten to do anything I was capable of."

John Green Brady, photographed in 1904. Brady started life as a foster kid but went on to become governor of Alaska (1897–1906).

THE MODERN ERA

Over time, individual states developed their own approaches to foster care. The first step toward a **federal** role was the Children's Bureau, which was created in 1912. The bureau's goal was to study and improve the welfare of all American children. Initially, it focused mainly on infant mortality and child labor problems. During the Great Depression, child welfare advocates hoped that antipoverty programs (as part of the "New Deal" programs) would also help kids. In particular, the Social Security Act of 1935 authorized the Children's Bureau to work more closely with states to help abandoned and neglected children.

Interestingly, technology played a role, too. Increased use of X-rays in hospitals allowed doctors to discover something that had gone unnoticed before: multiple fractures in the bones of young children. X-rays made the physical abuse of children much harder to ignore.

In 1962 an article was published in the *Journal of the American Medical Association* called "Battered Child Syndrome." The authors declared that doctors

Funding Priorities

Imagine that the government decides to give one dollar per week to every kid who plays trumpet in the school band. But it will only give 25 cents to kids who play clarinet. What do you think will happen? Before long, schools will have very big brass sections and very small woodwind sections. And that's how the government creates **incentives**.

If states are rewarded financially for putting kids in foster care, the reward makes them more likely to do so. If, on the other hand, they are rewarded financially for putting biological families back together, they might be more likely to do that. It is especially difficult for teenage foster kids to get adopted. So new incentives were created in 2014 to reward states that got more of their older kids into permanent homes. Critics still argue, however, that incentives should focus more on reunification rather than adoption.

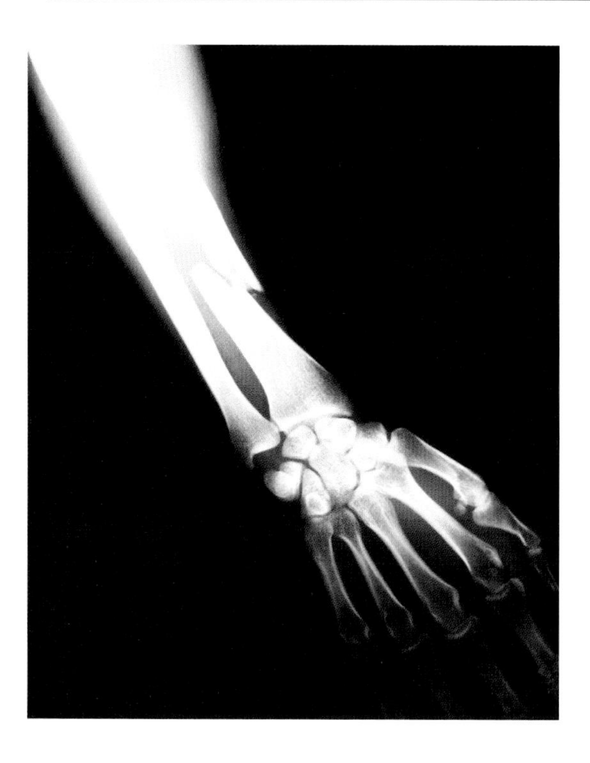

Medical X-rays made broken bones impossible to ignore; this in turn made doctors more aware of child abuse.

had a responsibility to intervene when they saw evidence of abuse. This gave fuel to the push for a more structured type of child protection and foster care. The Child Abuse Prevention and Treatment Act became law in 1974. The law created the National Center on Child Abuse and Neglect (NCCAN) and provided federal support to state efforts to prevent, report, and prosecute child abuse.

Since the mid 1970s, both state and federal laws have been written (and rewritten) to create the foster system we have today. Many people now feel that earlier laws kept too many kids in foster care. Both states and private agencies received federal funding based on the number of foster kids they served. This created financial incentives to keep kids in the system.

Since the 1990s, the focus on adoption has increased. Getting kids adopted by new parents—either their foster parents or extended family members (kinship care)—is seen as a better option. Today, funding tends to reward **permanence**. Funding is tied to success in adoption, rather than to keeping kids in foster care. This is an improvement, but critics would still like to see the incentives adjusted. They argue that the government should do more to reward reunification (getting families back together) rather than adoption.

Text-Dependent Questions

1. Why was the Orphan Train movement created?
2. What does the Indian Child Welfare Act have to do with foster care?
3. How did X-rays influence the development of the foster care system?

Research Project

Research pictures of the Orphan Train online and create a collage with captions explaining the details of each image you find. If you don't have access to the Internet, write three to four journal entries, imagining yourself on an Orphan Train being sent to a new place and family, based on what you've learned in the chapter.

As part of a "home study," a social worker interviews a potential foster family, to make sure they can provide a good home to foster kids who need one.

Chapter Three

TYPES OF FOSTER CARE

Foster care services are managed by special **agencies** in each state. The specific names vary, but the agencies are usually called the "Department of Children and Family Services" or something similar. These agencies work with both state-run homes and private firms to help place foster kids in homes and manage their cases. Each family usually has a social worker, or "case manager," who helps them understand what is happening and what needs to happen next. While parents deal with whatever problems they may have, kids are placed into one of these types of living situations: foster families, kinship care, or group homes.

Words to Understand

agencies: departments of a government with responsibilities for specific programs.

background check: a process that involves looking at a person's past, including criminal and financial records.

stipend: a small payment.

FOSTER FAMILIES

When people think of "foster care," they usually think of a regular home where a mother and father take in foster kids and raise them as their own. Some families only take in foster kids for short periods, while others are open to keeping them for long periods or even adopting them permanently. Foster families usually receive some sort of **stipend** from the state, to help pay for the care of the child (see sidebar).

To become a foster parent, an adult must meet a set of criteria set by the state. Every state writes its own requirements for who can foster a child. For example, some states require that only legally married couples can apply to foster children, but others do not. All states do require some kind of

Some states require that foster parents complete a first-aid class before they can take in any kids.

In It for the Money?

To encourage families to take in foster kids, states give money to foster parents to help with expenses. Rates vary depending on the state and the age of the child involved: Alabama pays around $100 per week, depending on the age of the child, while the Maryland average is around $180 per week. Children who are sick or have special needs are often more expensive to care for, and so states may pay additional stipends in those situations. A 2012 study compared the actual cost of raising kids to the stipends given to foster families. The study found that the majority of states paid far *less* than what it actually costs to house and feed a child—some paid less than half of the expected real costs.

One stereotype of foster parents is that they are "only in it for the money." There's not a great deal of logic to this "only for the money" idea, however. Caring for a child is a tremendous amount of work and responsibility. There are *much* easier ways to earn $100 per week! Yes, there are unscrupulous people everywhere, and scams do happen. But in general, foster parents do what they do because they want to share their love and attention with kids who are in trouble.

background check on everyone who lives in the home, but what that background check involves can vary by state. A background check is usually part of a larger "home study," in which professionals take a close look at the person or couple who would like to foster a child. The home study allows foster care officials get to know the families and find out what kind of child would fit them best. Foster-care home studies are similar—and sometimes identical—to home studies that adoptive parents undergo. (For more on adoption, see the volume *Adoptive Families* in this set.)

Most states require that would-be foster parents pass some type of official course or training program. They have to learn about child development, safety, and psychological challenges of foster kids, among other topics. Some states have even more specific rules: some require that the parents pass a first-aid course, while North Dakota expects that foster parents be trained about fire prevention.

States also write their own regulations about foster homes—specific rules include the number of bedrooms and bathrooms, level of cleanliness, the presence of smoke detectors and/or fire extinguishers, and so on. As of 2013, the majority of states forbade smoking in the presence of foster kids.

KINSHIP CARE

The word *kin* refers to an extended family—grandparents, uncles and aunts, cousins, and so on. *Kinship care* means that a foster child stays (either temporarily or for a long time) with members of their extended families. (Another term, *relative placement*, means the same thing as kinship care.)

Many child welfare advocates are pushing for kinship care to replace stranger care as often as possible. The fact that kinship care is "trendy" is somewhat ironic, because the idea of an extended family stepping in to help a child is as old as humanity. Especially in Hispanic and African-American communities, close-knit extended families are not a new trend. That's simply the way life is meant to be lived.

Kinship care can be a casual arrangement that does not involve government agencies. Sometimes families work out child care and custody among themselves, without getting social workers involved. Other times, kinship care is more formal—in that case, it's often called *kinship foster care*. In that situation, the relative is licensed as a foster parent and is subject to the same oversight that any other foster parent would be.

Because these arrangements can often be casual, it's not always easy to count how many kids live this way. It is estimated that there are about 2.4 million

When "foster parents" are biologically related to the kids, that's called kinship care.

caregivers who were responsible for a relative's child. The most common type of kinship care is when a child lives with a grandparent. Several studies have indicated that children in kinship care have fewer emotional problems and are less likely to run away than children who are fostered by strangers. They are also less likely to be adopted—probably because the caregiver is already a relative.

One down side of kinship care, at least where grandparents are concerned, is that grandparents tend to be poorer and less educated than their children. Also, they are at greater risk of health problems, which can make caring for themselves *and* their grandchildren very challenging. But in general, child welfare advocates say that remaining connected to family members is better for most kids than being sent to live with strangers.

GROUP HOMES

A group home is a facility for unrelated people who need particular care. For example, there are group homes for people with severe disabilities, and there are also group homes for people recovering from drug problems. A group foster home, on the other hand, usually has 6 or more kids who can't live with their parents for some reason. Group homes are sometimes also referred to as "institutional care."

For the most part, group homes do not offer the kind of "family feel" that other types of foster care offer. Because many people live all together, group homes tend to have very strict rules that everyone must follow all the time. This can be difficult for foster kids, especially teenagers. Also, the people who work in

Some group homes have a "house parent" who lives with the kids all the time.

institutions do so as their jobs. They might be wonderful people, but their relationships with the foster kids may not be as close as those of family members or foster parents.

Jeremy Kohomban, who runs a group home in New York State called Children's Village, says, "We can help kids who were traumatized—we can stabilize you, treat you. But we can't teach you to be a brother [or] a sister." Kohomban believes that group homes are best used for short-term emergency situations.

But some group homes do try to build a family atmosphere as much as possible. For example, the Coyote Hill Christian Children's Homes in Missouri have "house parents" who live with residents full time. While the whole situation may not be ideal, there are good group homes out there. The trouble, of course, is finding space. Almost by definition, the best group homes are small, focusing on a limited number of kids at a time.

Text-Dependent Questions

1. What is the basic process for becoming a foster parent?
2. What is kinship foster care?
3. Why is kinship care more popular than group homes?

Research Project

Research fostering requirements in your state. What kind of requirements are there? Choose a couple of other states and research how rules are the same or different. Why do you think that would be? To get started, try the Adopt US Kids website (http://www.adoptuskids.org/for-families/state-adoption-and-foster-care-information), which has information on all 50 states plus U.S. territories.

Terminating parental rights is a sad thing, but it also paves the way for foster kids to find new families who will love and support them.

Chapter Four

ISSUES IN FOSTER CARE

Foster care is not supposed to be permanent. As discussed earlier, reunification is by far the first-choice outcome for most foster kids.

Unfortunately, not everybody gets his or her first choice. For one thing, not all parents are up for the challenge of addressing their issues. They may not be willing to get treatment for a drug problem, or they may not be able to stay clean. Some problems are just not fixable. Sometimes people are so damaged themselves that they can't stop hurting others—it may never be safe to live with them, no matter what.

In these cases, the best solution may be what's called *termination of parental rights*. That's when parents sign away all legal claims. In the eyes of the law, they become strangers to their child at that point. Termination sounds awful, and in a way it certainly is. But it can also be a good thing, because it paves the way for

Words to Understand

limbo: a state of transition or change.

supervised: overseen by someone else.

transitional: moving from one condition to the next.

traumas: extremely upsetting events.

adoption. It is pretty common for a foster family, which is temporary, to become an adoptive family, which is permanent.

While we wish it wasn't true, some foster kids don't get that happy ending, either. Some kids are moved again and again, going from group home to foster family to new foster family and so on. They get stuck in a kind of **limbo**—they don't get adopted, but they can't go home. It is not easy to grow up in long-term foster care.

CHALLENGES FOR TEENS

Many foster kids have seen things or had experiences that we wish no child had to experience. Those **traumas** are sometimes made worse by the uncertainty of being in foster care. The child advocate and former foster kid Jackie Hammers-Crowell wrote, "Foster kids think about moving all the time. . . . I never let myself get excited about family vacations until just before they happened because in the back of my mind I knew I might move by then."

Teenage foster kids sometimes have trouble doing something that other kids take for granted, like finding someone to teach them to drive.

Tips for Foster Youth

This advice comes from California's Office of Foster Care. You can find more on their website (http://www.fosteryouthhelp.ca.gov/10facts.html).

Play an active part in decisions about your life:

- You have the right to attend your court hearings.
- You have the right to see your case file.
- You also have the right to keep your file private.

Know what's available for you:

- Even if you age out, you still can get health insurance.
- There is also money available to help you continue your education.
- Talk to your case worker about what opportunities are out there.

Know your rights:

- You have the right to school and to after school activities.
- You have the right to talk to judges and lawyers about your case.
- You have the right to medical care and counseling if you need it.
- No one has the right to abuse you, physically or verbally.

Although life "in care" is never easy, it can be especially tough for teenagers. First of all, it's harder for teens to get placements with foster families. This leaves more teenagers stuck in group homes. Many states have passed laws that try to encourage more foster placements for teens. But still, many of them face long waits for a "real home."

Meanwhile, a lot of things that "average" teenagers take for granted are hard for foster kids. It's tough to get a driver's license, for example, if there is no car to practice on and no adult to help you learn. While "average" teens have parents to buy them the latest gear, foster kids might not be able to afford anything beyond the essentials. Staying in touch with friends through social media is practically a requirement for every teen these days, but if you can't afford your own phone or tablet, that's a lot harder to do.

Many teenagers get part-time jobs to pay for things they want. But it's tough to get and keep a job if you can't drive or if you keep getting moved around. Dating is also tricky, for a few reasons. Group homes have extremely strict rules and may not let kids date at all. Plus, a lot of kids in foster care didn't have good role models to begin with. They may not know what a good relationship looks like in the first place.

PARENTAL VISITS

As discussed earlier, reunification is a key goal of the foster system. Even when that's not possible, experts believe that most kids should have some contact with their birth parents. Studies have shown that foster kids who keep in contact with their biological family have less depression and anxiety, and also fewer behavioral problems. For that reason, court-ordered visits between parents and kids are pretty

It's not uncommon for courts to order visitation between biological parents and their children in foster care.

Length of Stay

In 2013, about 280,000 kids left foster care. According to Children's Bureau statistics, this is the amount of time they spent "in care":

- less than one month: 11 percent
- 1 to 11 months: 35 percent
- 12 to 23 months: 27 percent
- 24 to 35 months: 13 percent
- 3 to 4 years: 9 percent
- 5 or more years: 5 percent

common. A court can order **supervised** or unsupervised visitation, depending on the specific situation.

Sometimes these visits can be great. Other times, however, they are pretty stressful for everyone involved. Birth parents may feel sad about not having their kids, or angry at "the system" for taking them away. Sometimes kids feel angry at their birth parents. Or they may feel torn between loyalty to their birth family and liking their foster family. A lot of times, though, kids just miss their parents and want to go home. Even if home was a scary place at times, it's still home to them.

ADOPTION AND GUARDIANSHIP

For kids who can't return to their biological parents, adoption is often an important goal. Sometimes a relative will foster a child and then transition into what's called a permanent guardian. (Guardianship is like adoption, except that it ends when the child turns 18.) Other kids are placed in homes with people who start off as strangers but end up as trusted family. Most foster families do not start out expecting to adopt. But, in time, they get attached to their foster kids, and they choose the adoption route.

In recent years, around 50,000 or so kids are adopted out of the foster system each year. About 55 percent or so (depending on the year) are adopted by their foster parents. Of the remainder, about 30 percent are adopted by relatives, and the remaining 15 or so percent are adopted by nonrelatives who also were not the foster parents. Adoption requirements vary by state, just like fostering requirements do. (For more on adoption, please see another volume in this set, *Adoptive Families*.)

PROBLEMS WITH ABUSE

The foster care system exists partly because there are parents who abuse or neglect their children. Unfortunately, there are also foster parents and group home employees who abuse or neglect the kids in their care.

Group homes were once infamous for abuse. It's not fair to accuse every group home of bad behavior, but it was more common in the past than it is today. There was very little oversight of group homes, and staffs were able to do

John Doe versus Giarretto

Child abuse is an uncomfortable subject, and we all wish it didn't happen. But sometimes mistakes are made, and foster kids are placed with bad people. In an extreme case in 2006, John Hardy Jackson was convicted of abusing so many foster kids that he was sentenced to 220 years in prison.

Four years later, one of the survivors brought a lawsuit against Jackson and the Giarretto Institute, the private agency that fostered him with Jackson. The survivor's lawyers argued that Jackson was never given a proper background check and that Giarretto ignored allegations of the abuse. The jury took one day to award the survivor $30 million. It was one of the largest settlements of its kind in California history.

pretty much they wanted. For instance, it used to be easy for group homes to take a certain amount of money from the government to pay for food, give far less food to their foster kids, and pocket the difference. This is a crime, and states have regulations in place to limit this kind of abuse. Meanwhile, child welfare advocates continue to push for stronger laws and more oversight.

The Children's Bureau, which is now part of the U.S. Department of Health and Human Services (HHS), tracks problems with foster care. In a 2012 report to Congress, the Children's Bureau found that only 0.3 percent of foster kids were found to have experienced "maltreatment" while in care.

The problem is, the overall percentage doesn't matter much if the abuse is happening to you. If it's happening to you, it is happening 100 percent. If you are being abused, there are phone numbers and websites at the back of this book that can connect you to people who would like to help.

AGING OUT

Every year, some kids pass the threshold of adulthood and are forced to leave the foster system. In 2013 about 23,000 kids "aged out" of foster care. The number of kids who reach adulthood (the age of 18) without a permanent family has crept up over the years—in 2002, only 8 percent of kids aged out of care; in 2013 the number was up to 10 percent.

A nice thing about going to college is that it provides a **transitional** period between being a teenager and a grown-up. College kids get to try living on their own, but in a safe way. While they might make some mistakes, the college environment is a sort of bubble, in which the punishment for most mistakes is not very high. Most kids who age out of foster care do not get the benefit of a transitional period. One day, they are 17 years old and in care; the next day, they are 18 and out of it.

Particularly for kids in group homes—as opposed to those with foster families who *might* be able to help them out a bit—aging out of the foster system can set young people on a path to disaster. A study published in 2010 found that only half of former foster kids have jobs by the time they are 24, and about 75 percent of the young women become pregnant. About 80 percent will be arrested, and 60 percent will be convicted of a crime. Twenty percent will be homeless at some point within just 18 months of aging out. A survey conducted by the California Department of Corrections found that 14 percent of inmates had been in foster care at some point in their lives.

Aging out usually occurs when someone reaches age 18. But there are efforts underway in some states to raise that age to as high as 21. In 2008, the U.S. Congress passed the Fostering Connections to Success and Increasing Adoptions Act. Among other things, the act offered additional funding to states that expand foster services until age 21. A few states have followed up with this idea, but many have not.

Unfortunately, about 20 percent of kids who age out of foster care spend some time on the streets.

People who age out of foster care don't just disappear. If they age out before they are ready to take care of themselves, they can *still* be expensive to society. They may need welfare, health care, policing, jails, and other services. Considering these expenses, a former foster kid could cost the state as much as $300,000. Some people argue that it's cheaper to teach kids more life skills in their early 20s than it is to keep them in prison after their bad choices are already made.

Opportunity Savings

The Jim Casey Youth Opportunities Initiative creates programs to help foster kids transition into adulthood. One program is called the Opportunity Passport. Starting as early as age 14, kids in foster care can get what's called a "matched savings account." Money that the young person saves is matched by donations from the project. Meanwhile, he or she takes classes to learn about money management and other finance-related topics. For example, someone who is planning to used matched savings to buy a car might get training in how to shop for cars, how to get insurance, and so on. (To find out more about the program, check out the initiative's website, at http://www.jimcaseyyouth.org/our-work-states, or do an Internet search on "Opportunity Passport" plus your state name, to see if there is a program near you.)

Text-Dependent Questions

1. What are some of the challenges faced by teens in foster care?
2. About how many foster kids are adopted every year?
3. What are some of the risks for kids who age out of foster care?

Research Project

Write a persuasive essay that either defends or critiques the idea of expanding foster care to age 21. When you prepare your text, consider what the "other side" would say, and attempt to disprove their argument.

FURTHER READING

Books

Accinelli, Therese. *My Lifebook Journal: A Workbook for Children in Foster Care.* Oakland, CA: Instant Help Books, 2008.

Family Care Network. *Lifebook: For Transitional Age Youth.* Santa Maria, CA: Family Care Network, 2012.

Harrison, Kathryn A. *Another Place at the Table.* New York: Jeremy P. Tarcher, 2003.

Online

Child Welfare Information Gateway. "Foster Care Statistics 2013." https://www.childwelfare.gov/pubPDFs/foster.pdf.

Fessler, Pam. "Report: Foster Kids Face Tough Times after Age 18." National Public Radio, *Morning Edition*, April 7, 2010. http://www.npr.org/templates/story/story.php?storyId=125594259.

Foster Care to Success. "Knowledge Center—Foster Care: The Basics." http://www.fc2success.org/knowledge-center/foster-care-the-basics/.

Get Help Now

Childhelp National Child Abuse Hotline

This free hotline is available 24-hours-a-day in 170 different languages.

1-800-4-A-CHILD (1-800-422-4453) http://www.childhelp.org

National Sexual Assault Hotline

Counselors can help sexual assault victims, their friends, and families.

1-800-656-HOPE (1-800-656-4673) https://ohl.rainn.org/online/

SERIES GLOSSARY

agencies: departments of a government with responsibilities for specific programs.

anxiety: a feeling of worry or nervousness.

biological parents: the woman and man who create a child; they may or not raise it.

caregiving: helping someone with their daily activities.

cognitive: having to do with thinking or understanding.

consensus: agreement among a particular group of people.

custody: legal guardianship of a child.

demographers: people who study information about people and communities.

depression: severe sadness or unhappiness that does not go away easily.

discrimination: singling out a group for unfair treatment.

disparity: a noticeable difference between two things.

diverse: having variety; for example, "ethnically diverse" means a group of people of many different ethnicities.

ethnicity: a group that has a shared cultural heritage.

extended family: the kind of family that includes members beyond just parents and children, such as aunts, uncles, cousins, and so on.

foster care: raising a child (usually temporarily) that is not adopted or biologically yours.

heir: someone who receives another person's wealth and social position after the other person dies.

homogenous: a group of things that are the same.

ideology: a set of ideas and ways of seeing the world.

incarceration: being confined in prison or jail.

inclusive: accepting of everyone.

informally: not official or legal.

institution: an established organization, custom, or tradition.

kinship: family relations.

neglect: not caring for something correctly.

patriarchal: a system that is run by men and fathers.

prejudice: beliefs about a person or group based only on simplified and often mistaken ideas.

prevalence: how common a particular trait is in a group of people.

psychological: having to do with the mind.

quantify: to count or measure objectively.

restrictions: limits on what someone can do.

reunification: putting something back together.

secular: nonreligious.

security: being free from danger.

social worker: a person whose job is to help families or children deal with particular problems.

socioeconomic: relating to both social factors (such as race and ethnicity) as well as financial factors (such as class).

sociologists: people who study human society and how it operates.

spectrum: range.

stability: the sense that things will stay the same.

stereotype: a simplified idea about a type of person that is not connected to actual individuals.

stigma: a judgment that something is bad or shameful.

stressor: a situation or event that causes upset (stress).

traumatic: something that's very disturbing and causes long-term damage to a person.

variable: something that can change.

INDEX

Page numbers in *italics* refer to photographs or tables.

ABOUT THE AUTHOR

H. W. Poole is a writer and editor of books for young people, including the 13-volume set, *Mental Illnesses and Disorders: Awareness and Understanding* (Mason Crest). She created the *Horrors of History* series (Charlesbridge) and the *Ecosystems* series (Facts On File). She has also been responsible for many critically acclaimed reference books, including *Political Handbook of the World* (CQ Press) and the *Encyclopedia of Terrorism* (SAGE). She was coauthor and editor of *The History of the Internet* (ABC-CLIO), which won the 2000 American Library Association RUSA award.

PHOTO CREDITS

Photos are for illustrative purposes only; individuals depicted are models.

Cover: Dollar Photo Club/Rob

iStock.com: 6 Mordorlff; 9 Den Kuvaiev; 12 abalcazar; 14 metinkiyak; 16 PeopleImages; 24 emmy-images; 36 Lorraine Boogich; 38 PeopleImages; 42 Stockphoto4u

Library of Congress: 18 Lewis Wickes Hine; 21 Bain News Service; 23 J.C. Strauss

Shutterstock: 26 Monkey Business Images; 28 Andrey_Popov; 31 Monkey Business Images; 32 Vital inka; 34 mimagephotography

Wikimedia Commons: 10 jdeeringdavis